pumpkin chic

COUNTRY LIVING

pumpkin chic

decorating with pumpkins and gourds

principal photography by Andrew McCaul

principal styling by Lauren Hunter

text by Mary Caldwell

HEARST BOOKS
A DIVISION OF STERLING PUBLISHING CO., INC.
NEW YORK

COUNTRY LIVING

pumpkin chic

Copyright © 2002 by Hearst Communications, Inc.

Produced by Smallwood & Stewart, Inc., New York City

Editor: Bruce Shostak
Designer: Linda Kocur

All photography by Andrew McCaul, except for the following: pages 4–5 and 17 by Roy Gumpel; pages 7 (middle) and 56 by Keith Scott Morton; pages 8, 10, 21, 25 (bottom right), and 82 by Steven Randazzo.

Library of Congress Cataloging-in-Publication Data
Available upon request.

10 9 8 7 6 5 4 3 2 1

Published by Hearst Books,
A Division of Sterling Publishing Co., Inc.
387 Park Avenue South, New York, N.Y. 10016

Country Living and Hearst Books are trademarks owned by
Hearst Magazines Property, Inc., in USA,
and Hearst Communications, Inc., in Canada.

www.countryliving.com

Distributed in Canada by Sterling Publishing
c/o Canadian Manda Group, One Atlantic Avenue, Suite 105
Toronto, Ontario, Canada M6K 3E7
Distributed in Australia by Capricorn Link (Australia) Pty. Ltd.
P.O. Box 704, Windsor, NSW 2756 Australia

Manufactured in China

ISBN 1-58816-095-5

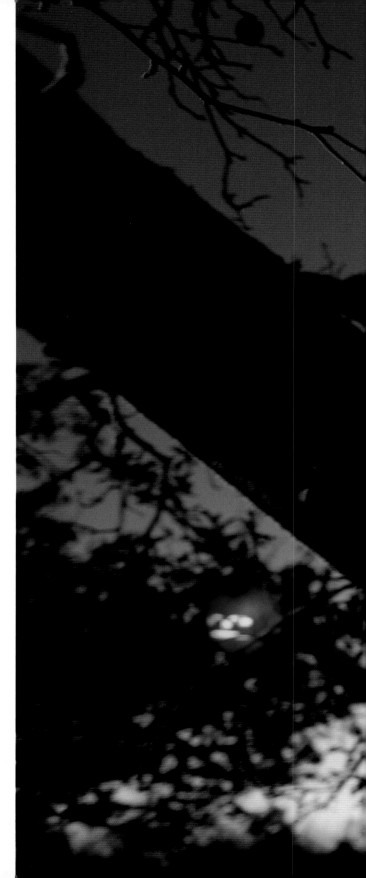

contents

introduction

What gives us joy in autumn, that season of colorful change, is that there's magic in it. The first flash of crimson leaves on a country lane, the excitement of planning a Halloween costume, and, yes, that first small orange pumpkin carried home from a market—maybe just a little bit too early for carving, but who can resist? These are the sweet highlights that capture the spirit around us.

This book is all about making the most of that pumpkin—and all of its squash and gourd cousins—in your seasonal decorating. Included are many inventive, out-of-the-ordinary jack-o'-lanterns. But here, too, are sophisticated and unusual ideas for using the farmstand's bounty to imbue your home with beauty all season long. Many pumpkins are illuminated from within, many etched only on the surface; some are so easy you'll want to launch an assembly line, while others take a bit more patience to complete. At the top of each project page, we indicate the spirit of the project: "quick concept" (truly *un*complicated), "artful touch" (adaptable and requiring some patience), "sum of its parts" (assembled materials), "uncarved features" (little or no carving required), and "autumn chic" (as at home in the city as in the country). Whether you choose to create a spooky pumpkin creature or a stylish gourd lantern, do read the first chapter, "The Basics," before digging in. We hope you'll be inspired to decorate, entertain, and celebrate with wonderful new twists on pumpkin carving and to create your own style of pumpkin chic.

the basics

The carving of the jack-o'-lantern has long been a Halloween custom in households where there are children, and with the increasing popularity of Halloween celebrations, the ritual is shared by adults and children alike. Beyond being transformed into jack-o'-lanterns, members of the viny genus *Cucurbita*—which includes pumpkins, gourds, and squashes—make wonderful decorating materials for the entire house, indoors and outdoors.

Legend holds that the Irish get credit for the jack-o'-lantern. Though renditions of the tale vary, it seems our grinning Jack evolved from lanterns carved out of turnips and carried in Celtic celebrations of the Day of the Dead. In recent years, pumpkin carving has evolved from crudely cut faces to sophisticated, intricate designs that are just as likely to become the centerpieces for a lovely dinner party as they are to liven up a round of trick or treating.

choosing what to carve

Pumpkins, the most traditional choice, range in size from the orange 'Jack Be Little' and the white 'Baby Boo' (each of which grows to no more than about three inches wide and two inches tall) to the mammoth prize-winning 'Atlantic Giant,' which can weigh in at over a whopping one thousand pounds.

The familiar orange pumpkin, a perennial favorite, is only one possibility for carving or decorating. Experiment with bumpy gourds, shapely speckled goosenecks, lantern-shaped specimens, and the Hubbard squash, whose ghostly green skin reveals a bright orange flesh.

But that's just the beginning. 'Kuri,' 'Kabocha,' 'Hokkaido,' 'Cushaw,' 'Lakota,' 'Delicata'—what sounds like a magical incantation is just a partial list of the many varieties of squash that are readily available today, joining the likes of acorn and butternut and the whimsical-sounding sweet dumpling. (All pumpkins and gourds are, technically, squashes.)

Hard-skinned winter squashes and gourds, such as acorn and butternut, require a bit more patience to carve, especially if the surface is prominently ridged or warty, but they can yield bewitching creations. Consider some of the stranger-looking species, too—for instance, the gooseneck gourd or the bumpy, pale blue-green-skinned Hubbard squash. Species with contrasting colors of skin and flesh, such as the white 'Lumina,' with its orange interior, will unleash the artist in you.

For best results, choose a specimen that has no soft spots or signs of mold or rot. Even if you intend to remove the stem, it's best to purchase a pumpkin with an intact stem, as the flesh is subject to quicker decay once the stem is broken. (To avoid accidents, never use the stem as a handle.) You don't necessarily need a "perfect" shape, however; surface bumps and quirky contours can all become integral to your design. Don't worry about caked-on dirt, either. Much of this can be easily removed with a stiff-bristled brush, a dampened sponge or rag, or a quick rinse under water.

planning the design

Pumpkins, squashes, and gourds hold practically unlimited potential for autumn and Halloween decorations. Go to the pumpkin patch with a design in hand and choose a

illuminating ideas

When lit from within, a jack-o'-lantern's persona emerges. Even the simplest designs look magical glowing in the dark, and any little "mistakes" will no longer matter.

candle power

Use candles safely. Place them only in steady pumpkins that won't be bumped or pose a hazard to children. A votive candle in a glass holder—or more than one, for brightness—or a taper candle that's become a bit stubby are the most reliable choices. To anchor a taper, scoop out a hole, drip a little melted wax into it, and immediately stick the candle in to secure it. Another trick is to cut a hole in the bottom of the pumpkin and slide the pumpkin over a candle. Light candles with a long fireplace match or a long electronic lighter.

electric power

A small flashlight or battery-operated pumpkin light (available with a steady or blinking beam) is a safe flame-free alternative; for a brighter glow, use more than one. You may wish to set the light on a square of folded plastic wrap to prevent it from becoming slimy.

Plug-in electric options include 25- to 40-watt bulbs in outdoor utility light sockets (great for thick pumpkins that need stronger illumination) and strands of outdoor Christmas lights (with these, you can create a pathway of luminaria). Choose red or green lights instead of white for extra eeriness. The new indoor/outdoor LED (light-emitting diode) strings of lights work well, too. To keep lights clean, cut the pumpkin's opening in the bottom and carve a narrow channel in the back of the base to allow the wire to escape without being pinched.

For lighting a pumpkin-filled porch, you can keep it classic with lanterns or hanging strings of carnival lights. For a jollier touch, especially great for kids, invest in strings of lights with bulb covers shaped like pumpkins or ghosts.

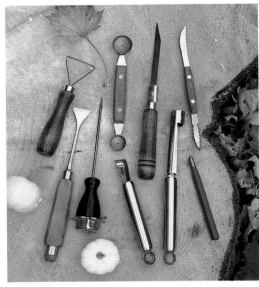

Carving a host of Halloween ghouls (opposite) might take several carvers several hours; if you choose a sole pumpkin, remember that the larger it is, the greater the effort and time required to prepare and carve it. For the work, kitchen knives and sturdy spoons are longtime standbys. Some other tools (top, left to right): potter's loop, chisel, awl, melon scoop, citrus zester, keyhole saw, apple corer, punch prick, and grapefruit knife. And other essentials (bottom, left to right): bamboo skewers for connecting parts, towel and brushes for cleanup, ice-cream scoop and pet-hair shedder for interior scraping, masking tape and china markers for outlining designs, and gardener's soil scoop for removing seeds and pulp.

suitable "canvas," or work the other way around and let the shape and character of a squash inspire you.

For freehand work, sketch the design onto the surface of the pumpkin. A china marker (grease pencil) or a gel pen works especially well for this task: Both write smoothly on the surface; any remaining traces can be wiped away with a damp cloth when you're done. You could also use a pencil, a ballpoint pen, or any pointed tool to etch the design in the surface. If you're using a paper stencil or template, tape it to the pumpkin and make a dotted outline in the skin with a pointed tool. Remove the paper and connect the dots as you carve.

gathering your tools

While pumpkin-carving tool kits are available commercially—at various levels of quality and cost—you can assemble a set to suit your personal preferences. You probably have almost everything you'll need in your toolbox and kitchen drawers. Numerous artists' and gardeners' implements can also be pressed into service. Experiment to see what works best for you.

An access hatch in the back of the pumpkin instead of a cut-out lid leaves the front of the pumpkin looking smooth; the notch eliminates guesswork when replacing the door.
A chimney vent that was power-drilled with a hole-cutter drill bit near the top lets candle smoke and heat escape.

Here are some suggestions for what to try:

+ for making cuts, a sharp paring knife, a thin boning knife, a curved-blade grapefruit knife, a utility knife, or a narrow serrated pumpkin saw; whichever you choose, remember that sharper is better—you won't have to apply as much pressure

+ for chiseling, a wood-carving tool, sculptor's tool, or even a flat-head screwdriver

+ for removing seeds and pulp, an ice cream scoop, serving spoon, potting scoop, or even a looped and serrated pet-shedding blade

+ for making chimney vents and decorative holes, an electric drill and an apple corer

+ for etching and inscribing, a citrus zester, linoleum cutter, or potter's tool

getting under way

Pumpkin carving is a messy business, but well worth it. Cover tables with newspaper and put out bowls or plastic bags to collect seeds, pulp, and carvings. As many veteran pumpkin carvers have found, precise chiseling and etching work is often easiest with the pumpkin resting steady in your lap; protect your clothing with a large utility towel.

For a pumpkin that will be illuminated from within, start by cutting an access hole. The traditional method is to carve a cap around the stem; it's easiest if you make an angular (e.g., octagonal) rather than a circular cutout. To prevent the cap from falling into the pumpkin, slant the cuts inward so that the lid will be wider at its top.

Another way to make an access hole is to cut a door in the back of the pumpkin, which leaves the front and top free for carving. Cut a door large enough for removal of the pulp

Once you settle on the most comfortable tools and apply a few cutting techniques, pumpkin carving lets you unleash your creative genius.

and the seeds, incorporating a notch in one side of the door so it will fit easily, like a puzzle piece; again, slant the cuts inward so the outside of the door is bigger than the inside. You may need to secure a back door in place with one or two toothpicks, floral u-pins, or cotter pins. If outdoor electric lights will be used, carve away a notch to leave a channel for the cord.

Hollowing out the pumpkin from the base suits some designs. The virtue of a base opening is that you can set the cut pumpkin directly over the lit candle instead of having to reach inside with a match; just be sure to protect surfaces against damage from the moist pumpkin.

Next, you'll need to clean out the inside of the pumpkin thoroughly. An ice cream scoop or a soil scoop manages the task well. If you wish, save the seeds, rinse them free of pulp, and roast them for a snack (recipe on page 87).

If you're going to burn a candle inside the pumpkin, you'll probably need a chimney vent for the escape of heat and smoke. Cut a triangular notch from the lid or, if you're using a back door or a base opening, a round hole behind the stem near the top of the pumpkin. For cutting chimney vents (or decorative holes) in pumpkins, an apple corer usually works fine. Use an electric drill fitted with a regular or hole-cutter bit to make quick work of multiple pumpkins and gourds that have very hard skin and flesh. Drill bits in various sizes will give you creative flexibility. Always wear protective goggles and exercise caution when drilling. Be sure the pumpkin is steady at all times.

Many designs call for scraping or chiseling away just a bit of the pumpkin, not cutting all the way through. This technique yields beautiful results that can be romantic or a bit spooky. If you're lighting a chiseled creation from the inside, you'll usually need to scrape away additional flesh from the inside of the pumpkin, making a thinner wall that reveals more of a glow.

Because most carving tools are basic and personal preferences abound (the same effect can be created using various tools), the instructions in this book list only the materials; specific tools or types of tools are suggested within the step-by-steps. Most projects can be adapted to various squashes, sizes, and interpretations, so feel free to use imagination and creativity as your guides.

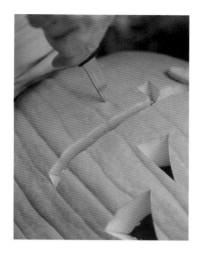

In pumpkin carving as in food preparation, a sharp knife is always safer than a dull one because less pressure is required to make a sure cut. Always work slowly and carefully; pull the blade out of the flesh and reinsert it at the new angle when changing your carving direction.

chapter 2

Creatures

scary and nice

Come October, when it's time to venture out to the pumpkin patch or browse a local farmstand, unleash your imaginative powers as you select the squashes to put on your operating table. Exactly what—or maybe even whom—does a particular pumpkin remind you of? Not that pumpkin-picking has to turn into an identification exercise, but an open-minded look at autumn produce may suggest a new world of scary, winsome, or amusing characters.

Start by looking beyond those perfectly round orange pumpkins. Lopsided and warty-surfaced specimens can become jack-o'-lanterns with distinctive personalities. White- or green-skinned pumpkins and all manner of hard-shelled winter squashes give you the chance to create otherworldly characters.

For beginners, a good choice is the triangle-eyed, maniacally grinning jack-o'-lantern. It certainly holds a place of honor in the pumpkin hall of fame. Straight lines and simple shapes, after all, are the easiest to execute. Without too much more effort or skill, however, you can easily carve or assemble innovative creatures that will elicit lots of smiles or shrieks—and compliments.

No rule says that a pumpkin must sit upright, presenting a face on its broadside and a curled stem for its topknot. Tip the pumpkin on its side and

Get in a ghostly spirit with classic jack-o'-lanterns, rakishly decorated stem-nosed imps, and a complement of seasonal supplies: perhaps some twigs, seedpods, berries, sunflower blooms, or a faux crow. With luck, maybe a prowling cat will arrive to provide instant inspiration.

On Halloween night, pumpkins and gourds may magically strive to animate themselves. Help them along with a chisel and a cut or two.

the stem is suddenly, unmistakably, a funny nose. Or maybe that stem is a creepy tail and the base of the pumpkin is the area that deserves a face. Hang a pumpkin upside down: The stem is the neck of a ghoulish head. A squash could serve as the body of a creature, rather than its head, with sticks for arms and legs. Another option is to use the surface as a canvas: Carve the outline, silhouette style, of a bat, a cat, or a spider. Or try your hand at an old-fashioned silhouette of a family member or ancestor.

Seasonal materials can also enhance the personality of your creation. Ears of Indian corn, strands of ivy, and other ingredients can become fearsome facial features or a pumpkin fright wig. Ask yourself what role your pumpkin will play? Is it a bloodthirsty vampire? Frankenstein's monster? A wicked witch? A funny-faced sprite or a circus clown? Then ask yourself what different elements might become under your creative direction. Does a crooked chile pepper, turned sideways, look like a sinister leer? Do kernels of Indian corn resemble beady bat eyes. Props come in handy, too, especially at Halloween, when theatricality is the order of the day. Heighten the effect of a display with some treasures from the attic or toolshed. And now, let your pumpkin don its finery.

eerie props and spooky add-ons

For sly or spectacular effects, your jack-o'-lantern can be embellished in many ways other than carving. To involve children who are too young to wield cutting tools, you can, of course, let them paint their own designs on pumpkins large and small (or let them mark designs for you to cut). But with some extra elements you can really dress up your gourd.

theatrical spirit

Think in terms of wardrobe and props. Find a pointy witch's hat or a straw garden hat from summers past to lend sinister charm or rustic flair to glowing faces. Let a toy arrow or an old scythe inspire the setting of a grim and gruesome tableau, set up for a frightful Halloween fete. Use artificial—and surprisingly convincing—crows, bats, rats, spiders, and spiderwebs (widely available in the weeks leading up to the holiday) to stage a spooky show. You'd be surprised: Even a single uncarved pumpkin with a faux blackbird perched on its stem has the power to playfully startle visitors when they catch a glimpse through the front window.

natural weirdness

Look in the garden, yard, and woods and at floral shops, garden centers, and the grocery store for natural add-ons. Twigs are spindly arms or eerie antennae. Leaves or corn husks, attached with floral u-pins, can look like a ruffled collar or a shaggy coiffure. Seedpods, which nature offers in such astonishing variety, are abundant this time of year; use them as eyes, horns, or even tongues. Try sumac pods, pinecones, broom corn fronds, or cattails—just carve a hole into which the materials will fit snuggly. Even gourds themselves can be the add-ons. Don't be afraid to cut them apart to make eyes, ears, noses, or whatever else you can envision hiding in their round or coiled shapes.

scar-faced monster

No doubt a kin of Frankenstein's infamous creature, this not-at-all-handsome fellow is a frightful assemblage of parts—including his visible brain. To make one like him, select a large, squarish pumpkin, preferably with bulges and blemishes. This jack-o'-lantern requires only the most basic carving techniques—the misshapen add-on features provide the special effects.

1. Cut a door in the back of the pumpkin and scoop out the seeds and pulp. Cut a chimney vent behind the stem near the top of the pumpkin.

2. With a marker, sketch the eyes, nose, and mouth. Plan carefully so the round gourds will fit snugly into the eye sockets and the corn will fit into the mouth. Cut the eyes, nose, and mouth. With a citrus zester or a potter's tool, score two lines under one eye to suggest a black eye. Wedge in the gourd eyeballs. Remove several kernels from the cob to simulate missing teeth, then wedge it into the mouth opening.

3. Mark and cut a hole on one side of the forehead to accommodate the cockscomb "brains" snugly. Trim the stems from the cockscomb, then wedge the bunch into place.

4. For ears, cut the third gourd into quarters; clean out two of them. Insert two toothpicks into one cut edge of each "ear"; attach both to the head. Trim the toothpicks if necessary.

5. Insert the candle or light and replace the door.

materials

1 large pumpkin

several stems of cockscomb

1 ear Indian corn, trimmed to desired length

3 small round gourds

toothpicks or bamboo skewers

candle or battery-operated light

hanging
tree
ghouls
Suspend these teasing, taunting
floating heads from tree limbs or porch rafters.
Because they aren't illuminated from within, they need no
tending and so can hang anywhere, waiting to shock visitors.
Acorn squashes and small pumpkins work equally well
for this upside-down treatment, where the stem suggests
a neck (Eek!) or a tail (Yuk!).

1. Working with the stem side of the pumpkin oriented downward, use a marker to draw triangular eyes. With a knife or a
   chisel, score the outline of the eyes about ¼ inch into the
   pumpkin. Chisel out the eyes, about a ¼ inch deep.

2. Draw a circle for the mouth a little bit smaller than the pod.
   Carve the mouth with an apple corer or a serrated knife.
   Press the seedpod into the hole. If necessary, scrape the edge
   of the hole to accommodate the pod.

3. Screw the hook into the base (now the top of the head). If
   you're using a thick screw hook, you may want to drill a pilot
   hole first to keep the pumpkin from splitting.

4. Hang the finished ghoul.

materials

small pumpkins or
acorn squashes

round seedpods
(or small pinecones
or unshelled walnuts)

oversized screw hook
or hook and eye

queen of the crows

Only a sorceress as commanding as she could call these black-feathered friends to nest in her tumbling ivy tresses. Scary skin (look for an extra-warty pumpkin) superbly sets off bulging lady-apple eyeballs, a twisting gourd-stem nose, and stern hot-pepper lips. This is a (nearly) no-carve character that's fun to create with children. Consider making a coven of variations!

1. Around the stem of the pumpkin, mark a circle about the same diameter as the diameter of the top of the ivy pot. Cut out the circle. Remove seeds and pulp from the inside of the pumpkin. Fit the potted ivy into the top of the pumpkin and arrange the ivy to resemble messy hair.

2. For the eyes, attach the lady apples to the pumpkin with toothpicks. For the nose, cut the neck off the gourd and attach it with toothpicks. For the mouth, attach the pepper with toothpicks or a floral u-pin.

3. To help support the hat's pointy shape, if necessary, stuff it with crumpled tissue or newspaper. Place the witch's hat on the head and anchor it to the pumpkin with floral u-pins. Perch the crows around the witch.

materials

1 large pumpkin

English Ivy plant in plastic pot

2 lady apples

toothpicks

1 small long-necked gourd

1 red chile pepper

black witch's hat and artificial crows (available from costume and party-supply stores)

tissue or newspaper

floral u-pins

a batty welcome

Hovering in the night air, these eerie flying mammals will guard the front door all through Halloween, yet each takes only minutes to make. Their white acorn-squash bodies and corn-husk wings will glow like ghosts in the darkness. Suspend them from a porch ceiling, the eaves of the house, or tree limbs—just be sure to keep their wings and fangs out of head-bumping range.

1. Work with the stem end of the acorn squash as the top. With a large nail, gouge the squash's skin to make two holes for the corn-kernel eyes. Press the kernels into the holes so they are secure. With an awl, pierce two holes for the fangs; pierce the holes so that the fangs will point up or down or in different directions, as desired. Cut a toothpick in half and insert the blunt ends into the holes for fangs.

2. If there is no stem, screw or drive the hook into the stem end of the squash.

3. For the wings, use scissors to cut a scalloped edge on one side of each of two corn husks. Make sure you have a left and a right wing. Fasten each wing to the back of the squash with brads or floral u-pins.

4. Tie twine—or monofilament, for invisibility—to the stem or the hook for hanging.

materials

white acorn squashes

husks and kernels from Indian corn

toothpicks

screw-in hooks or drive hooks

brads or floral u-pins

twine or monofilament

space-alien ghosts

Weird periscope eyes give a pale family of ghosts distinctly sci-fi-in-the-country style. The fun of a display like this is in making each creature a bit different: tiny mouth, big mouth; one eye, two eyes. Let them peer out of windows, around corners, or from the rail of a fence. Or group them on the front steps, glowing amid several votives or lanterns at dusk.

1. Cut or break off the stem of each 'Lumina' pumpkin, if desired, or leave attached as an antenna.

2. With an apple corer or a drill fitted with a large bit, rout out circular mouths on the fronts of the pumpkins. Make the mouths in different sizes, if desired.

3. With the apple corer or drill, make one or two small eye sockets (depending on whether your alien is destined for Cyclopean or binocular vision) on each pumpkin. Trim the seedpod stems to a few inches and insert one into each opening.

4. For the votive holders, cut an opening that is the width of a candle into the top of each 'Baby Boo'; because they are very hard, it will be easier to cut a square opening using four straight cuts (this is a case of round pegs in square holes). Scoop out the seeds and the pulp and insert a candle.

materials

'Lumina' pumpkins

water lily seedpods

'Baby Boo' pumpkins and white gourds

votive candles

grim-
reaper
skull

Bewa-a-a-a-are the toolshed. Someone's ready for a little skulduggery with the implement of his trade. Most butternut squashes are pear shaped, which makes them perfect for transforming into skulls. But because butternut flesh is so thick and dense, carve with patience and extra care, working on a small section at a time.

1. Working with the stem of the squash pointing downward, to suggest neck vertebrae, lightly outline the eyes, nasal openings, and mouth with a marker. With a potter's tool or a citrus zester, scrape away the skin and some of the flesh to define the eye sockets and pupils, as shown. Work in a circular pattern; let the ridged texture of the carving show.

2. With a paring knife, carefully cut out the nasal openings; two curved and angled cuts, about $\frac{1}{2}$ inch deep, will be enough to define each one.

3. With a paring knife or a wood chisel, carve the mouth, removing small sections at a time. Carve as deeply as you can.

4. Cut a door in the back near the stem end. Work patiently. Scrape out the seeds and carve until the mouth is open all the way through. Trim and neaten the edges of the mouth opening as needed.

5. Screw the hook into the crown of the skull. If you're using a thick screw hook, you may want to drill a pilot hole first to keep the squash from splitting. Hang the skull.

materials

large, wide butternut squash

large screw-in hook

sumac-
horned
demon
Frowning with his own inner darkness (he's too small for a candle), this little devil has more fright than bite. You might enlist him to stand guard over a threatened plate of holiday treats. If you don't have sumac pods for his horns, try using red frying peppers or red chile peppers.

1. Cut a door in the back of the squash and remove the seeds and the pulp.

2. With a marker, draw the outlines of the mouth, eyes, and eyebrows. Cut out the eyes and the mouth.

3. With a linoleum cutter or a potter's tool, make the eyebrows by carving away just the skin and a small amount of flesh.

4. With a punch prick or drill, create two holes for the horns, making them almost as wide as the pod stems are thick, for a tight fit. Insert the sumac pod stems into the holes.

5. Replace the back door.

materials

'Golden Nugget' squash or small squat pumpkin

2 sumac pods

decorating
✦

sentry style
An easy way to infuse the whole house with Halloween is to carve many little jack-o'-lanterns, some with eyes only, and let them keep watch from tables, transoms, bookcases, nightstands, mantels, kitchen shelves, and other nooks and ledges. Leave some unlit—they're surprisingly devilish when they're dark within.

three little spirits

Who says the stem must stand straight up in the air? That's probably not the way these fellows were growing in the field. Prop a gourd on its side and the stem becomes a wonderfully expressive nose, perfect for a comic—or spooky—effect. Nuts, pinecones, pods, and berries can all become eyes. These spooks are lilliputian, but you could make giant ones, too.

1. Turn each pumpkin on its side with the stem facing toward you, then rotate it until you have the nose positioned to your satisfaction. If you wish, carve a small mouth just a little bit into the flesh with a linoleum cutter or a small knife. Be careful: Small gourds can be extremely hard.

2. Attach the eyes with hot glue. Lean the finished ghosts into position on a windowsill or shelf.

materials

'Baby Boo' and other tiny white gourds, with stems

acorns, berries, seedpods, or other small natural "eyes"

hot-glue gun

carving

◆

longer lasting

A pumpkin that has a design carved into its surface but isn't hollowed out will last longer than a traditional jack-o'-lantern. If you're saving sugar pumpkins for pies or soups, they can still become little monsters for Halloween: Tip them on their sides and gouge out two eyes and a mouth around the stem nose. Some carvers suggest rubbing a jack-o'-lantern's cut edges with a little petroleum jelly to seal in moisture. To rehydrate a slightly shriveled one, soak it in water for a few hours.

sunny-eyed smile

The long, thick eyelashes and happy disposition of this cheerful spirit virtually fly in the face of any Halloween haunting. Vials of water hidden inside the pumpkin keep the sunflower blossoms perky, no matter how late the party goes; use daisies on a smaller pumpkin.

1. Cut out a door in the back of the pumpkin and remove the seeds and the pulp. With a marker, outline the nose and mouth and cut them out.

2. Holding the flower stem pointing downward, remove several petals from the right and left sides of each flower, leaving the remaining petals to resemble eyelashes. Hold the flowers up to the pumpkin and mark the two spots where the stems will slip into the pumpkin. With an apple corer, punch out the two holes for the stems. Cut the flower stems and slip them through the holes. Reach in through the door and slip the stems into water-filled florist's vials.

3. Insert the candles or the light and replace the door.

materials

1 large round pumpkin

2 sunflowers or similarly petaled flowers

2 florist's vials

votive candles or battery-operated light

masked goblin partygoer

Not until midnight will identities be revealed! Autumn leaves of various shapes, sizes, and hues—instead of feathers and sequins—dress up a plain black mask; the black ribbon band hides the slice of the pumpkin's lid. Make a matching mask for yourself, dress in orange, and your party costume is complete.

1. Cut a lid from the top of the pumpkin, making the cut where you want the eyes to be, and remove the seeds and the pulp. Cut a chimney vent near the top of the back side of the pumpkin.

2. Place the lid on the pumpkin. Hold the mask up to the pumpkin, eyes centered on the slice of the lid. Trace the eye holes with a marker. Also mark the wide, grinning mouth. Cut out the top and bottom halves of the eyes from the body and lid of the pumpkin, and cut out the mouth.

3. Cut a piece of ribbon about 1½ feet longer than the circumference of the lid, cut it in half, and staple each piece to each side of the mask. Set the mask on a work surface and arrange the leaves. Glue the leaves to the mask.

4. Insert the two candles, the taper to provide light near the eyes, and the votive candle for light below the mouth.

5. Position the mask over the eye openings and attach it with floral u-pins where the ribbon meets the mask. Wrap the ribbon to the back and tie in a knot or a bow.

materials

very large, tall, bulbous pumpkin

black eye mask

wide black ribbon

assorted autumn leaves

craft glue or hot-glue gun

floral u-pins

tall taper candle

votive candle

wink and a smirk

If you're lucky enough to pick your pumpkin from the field—or from your own garden—instead of from a crate, you'll have a much better chance of finding a genuinely unusual specimen. When you do, make the most of an oddity and incorporate it into the design: This pumpkin began to grow around its own stem, resulting in a charming spit curl and a ready-made nose.

1. Cut out a door in the back of the pumpkin. Scoop out the seeds and the pulp. With an apple corer or a drill, cut a vent hole behind the stem near the top of the pumpkin.

2. Mark the facial features. In this case, the prominent crease in the pumpkin suggested a nose, so no nose was carved. Cut out the eyes—for the winking eye, cut only part of the way through the flesh on the bottom half of the eye, as shown. Cut out the mouth.

3. Insert the candle into the pumpkin; replace the back door.

materials

large pumpkin

candle

entertaining
◆

carving party

Pumpkin carving is a happily messy endeavor, to be sure. That's why it makes the most sense to host a carving party outdoors, weather permitting. Plan on starting a few hours before dusk, serve thermoses of warm cider and treats, have sweaters and woolen throws on hand, and, as the sky darkens, light everyone's masterpieces.

scaredy-cat profile

For basic jack-o'-lantern faces, all but the most timid carvers may want to freehand-sketch the outlines directly onto the pumpkin—or even carve first and think later. For more precise shapes, like this howling, yowling, meowling feline silhouette, it's best to draw the design on paper and then transfer it to the surface of the pumpkin.

1. Sketch the design on paper or photocopy this picture, enlarging it to the desired size.

2. Tape the pattern to the pumpkin. With a pointed tool, poke closely spaced holes through the outline and into the pumpkin's flesh. Remove the pattern.

3. Cut a door in the back of the pumpkin. Scrape out the seeds and the pulp.

4. Cut out the cat outline, connecting the dots.

5. For the standing-on-end hairs: Cut some hairs with a linoleum cutter, going only part of the way into the flesh; cut others by making two closely angled cuts with a paring knife, cutting all the way through.

6. Insert the candle and replace the back door.

materials

medium to large
squarish pumpkin

candle

arachnoid
web
site

It will certainly take some time, but this intricate spiderweb is actually quite easy to carve. Once you've marked the pattern with masking tape, cut and chisel everything that's not the web, leaving a thin layer of golden flesh to glow. Carve a creepy-crawly spider on another pumpkin, and the unsightly scene is set.

1. Cut a door into the back of each pumpkin. Scrape out the seeds and the pulp. Cut a vent hole behind the stem of each pumpkin.

2. With the masking tape, make a cross that covers the face of the larger pumpkin, then make the same sized "X" over the cross. Make concentric octagons that connect the arms of the web with smaller lengths of tape.

3. Cut and chisel away the areas of flesh between the tape, leaving about 1/4 to 1/2 inch of flesh.

4. For the spider, mark the outline on the front of the smaller pumpkin. Use a narrow knife or a saw to cut out the design; carve all the way through the pumpkin.

5. Set candles or lights in both pumpkins and replace the back doors. You will probably need several candles to illuminate the spiderweb; if it does not glow sufficiently, scrape away more of the flesh from the inside, being careful not to make a hole in the panels of the web.

materials

large pumpkin

small pumpkin

3/4-inch masking tape

candles or battery-
operated lights

shifty-
eyed
snouts
Every Hubbard squash, with its bluish green skin and peculiar form, definitely has a menacing critter inside. Carve as many of these antennae-sprouting creatures as you like and let them keep watch, peering this way and that, to ward off spirits more ghastly than they. There are no airholes for flames, so use battery-operated lights inside.

1. Cut a door from the bottom rear of each squash and scrape out the seeds and the pulp. You will need to thin the walls behind where the eyes will be—the thinner the flesh, the brighter the glow.

2. Mark the half-moon outlines of the eyes. Then mark smaller curves within the eyes for the pupils, making sure that each critter is looking in a different direction. With a paring knife or a utility knife, cut 1/4 to 1/2 inch, straight down, all the way around the outer outlines of the eyes. With a linoleum cutter or a small chisel, scrape away the skin and 1/4 to 1/2 inch of flesh for the whites of the eyes, leaving the skin within the pupil outlines intact.

3. Drill two small holes into the top of each head. Insert twigs into holes to form antennae.

4. Insert a battery-operated light or an electric lightbulb inside each squash, positioning it beneath the eyes (it should sit on the interior floor of the squash).

materials

Hubbard squashes

long twigs

battery-operated lights or outdoor-approved light sockets with 25- to 40-watt bulbs

faceless

pumpkins

Though uttering the very word "pumpkin" quickly invokes the image of Halloween jack-o'-lanterns, it's satisfying to carve stylish pumpkins without the usual eyes-nose-mouth references. Instead of conjuring up grinning ghouls or fiendish faces, look around for other inspiration. Autumn leaves, feathery fern fronds, shapely orchard fruit, or the heavens above are but starting points for patterns you can adapt and transfer to the surface of a pumpkin.

The lines of a column, a pediment, barn doors, or other architectural details could kindle a bold motif. Or perhaps you fancy the baroque curves of a chandelier or the profile of an antique garden urn. Visualize the shape pared down to its essential outline, perhaps carved in a repeating cycle. Think positive and negative, anticipating the glow of the finished pumpkin: Will you carve out the shape itself, or will you pare away a frame that surrounds it?

Household textiles are also a good source of motifs. Quilters have long used repeated geometric shapes to make a whole that's definitely more than the sum of its many patches. The basic triangle, traditionally used for jack-o'-lantern eyes and arguably the easiest shape to carve, takes on an entirely new dimension when duplicated and spiraled around a pumpkin or carved in an all-

Apply repeated motifs or perform a few tricks of the eye, and you can turn a pumpkin into a lovely utilitarian object— a pretty lantern, for example—or a wonderful work of folk art. Where is your inspiration? A family heirloom quilt, an etched-glass hurricane lamp, an antique carved finial?

Simple abstract patterns and clever trompe l'oeil effects introduce an artistic inventiveness to the pumpkin-carving craft.

over pattern. Flip through quilting books, examine textiles around the house, or experiment with your own designs on graph paper to arrive at a pleasing series of shapes. Maximize the interplay of form and pattern. How would the classic "Tumbling Blocks" look reproduced on a pumpkin? Or maybe a Victorian fan design, alternating carved and outlined segments? Even plain little circles, easily bored with a power drill or an apple corer, make a lively decorative scheme when illuminated from within.

Whatever the inspiration, variations for carving patterns are myriad. Combine shapes or choose one motif to repeat; carve one large image and many smaller echoes; align the patterns in stripes, a neat grid, or a free-floating array. Carve all the way through the flesh to achieve the traditional glow-from-the-interior illumination, or pare some of the design more or less skin-deep for a subtler kind of glow. If you don't wish to carve deeply, you can even etch a design on the surface for a pretty effect that won't require any interior lighting at all. This tooled approach is especially effective when the skin and flesh contrast in color, as in the case with a 'Lumina' pumpkin (white skin, orange flesh) or a butternut squash (tan skin, orange flesh).

photographing
the glow

It's fun to record each autumn's pumpkin masterpiece on film. Here are some tips for great results:

lights, please

Reconsider your instinct to photograph in the black of night. When the only light comes from within the pumpkin, you will capture the glowing cutouts but lose the pumpkin itself. For best effect, shoot the pumpkin outside in low natural light, at dawn or dusk.

Harsh exterior light can ruin the effect in a jack-o'-lantern photo. Avoid using a flash, which bounces hard light off the pumpkin's glossy surface, creating "hot spots." If your camera has a built-in flash that you can't override, cover the flash with your hand. For a moodier shot, hold a "curtain" of scrim or other sheer fabric (out of camera view) between the light source and the pumpkin to diffuse some of the brightness and reduce glare.

If you're shooting indoors, position the subject near natural light and in front of an attractive background. When natural light is not available, illuminate the pumpkin from above with a single light source, letting it angle down toward the front of the pumpkin.

places, everybody

Shoot at the pumpkin's level—just as you would if you were photographing children—getting in as close as your lens will permit. If the pumpkin is on the ground, stretch yourself out on the ground, too. If the pumpkin is on the front steps, set the camera on a low tripod. Depending on the pumpkin's size, you may need to increase the candle or bulb power inside for a brighter interior. Make sure the candle's glow, but not the flame itself, will show when you shoot.

And finally, don't skimp on processing. If you feel you've captured a nice shot but the print quality seems to be inferior, take your negative to a professional lab.

falling autumn leaves

Gather a collection of shapely leaves from the yard, a park, or the woods—maple, oak, and beech, for example—and use them as templates for this delicately tooled work of art. The technique, in fact, can be applied to almost any pumpkin, squash, or gourd. Use your results as a lunch-table centerpiece, a porch-bench decoration, or a gift for a neighbor.

1. Trace the outlines of the leaves onto the paper. Cut out a rectangle surrounding each leaf outline, as shown above.

2. Select the placement for one leaf at a time on the pumpkin and tape it into place. Use a ballpoint pen or a punch prick to trace over the leaf outline, scoring it into the surface of the pumpkin. Remove the paper and repeat with the other leaf outlines all around the pumpkin. You'll probably want to repeat the same outline several times on the same pumpkin.

3. With a linoleum cutter, carve the leaf outlines into the flesh, going over each outline only once. Add lines to mimic the actual veins on the leaves.

materials

medium to large squash

assorted leaves

plain paper

tape

plucked-
pear
illusion
Every fruit of the autumn harvest goes well together in fall arrangements. Here, the idea is reduced to its essentials: A Bosc pear seems to have been plucked from this 'Melonette St. Julien' squash to make a shapely sculpture. Choose a squash and a pear that are in nice proportion to each other. This squash's green flesh and pale golden skin complement the pear.

1. Break off the stem of the pumpkin.

2. By sight, mark the outline of the pear and its stem on the pumpkin. Or, if you prefer, slice a similar pear in half vertically, place it cut side down on the paper, and trace around it. Tape the pattern to the pumpkin and, with a ballpoint pen or a punch prick, trace over the pear outline, scoring the line into the surface of the pumpkin. Remove the paper.

3. With a paring knife or a utility knife, carefully cut straight into the pumpkin, following the outline of the pear and the stem, cutting about $\frac{1}{8}$ inch deep or a bit more. With a chisel or a similar tool, scrape away the skin and $\frac{1}{8}$ inch or so of the flesh within the outline. Smooth the cut surface of the flesh with your fingers for an even finish.

4. Insert half of the toothpick into the bottom of the pear. Attach the pear to the pumpkin by pressing the other half of the toothpick into the top of the pumpkin. If necessary, use an awl to make a pilot hole in the pumpkin's stem end.

materials

medium pear-shaped squash

Bosc pear with stem attached

toothpick

quilt-banded centerpieces

Look around the house: A quilt, a vintage printed tablecloth, or a wallpaper border could be your inspiration. This pair of country classics features positive/negative motifs borrowed from antique quilts. The designs are chiseled only into the surface, so these sophisticated table decorations are long-lasting.

1. For these designs, a checkerboard pattern repeats around the pumpkin, alternating in a positive/negative image. Mark three parallel, evenly spaced lines around the circumference of each pumpkin. Draw evenly spaced vertical lines from the top line to the bottom line to create a series of squares.

2. For the smaller, diamond motif, use a paring knife or a utility knife to cut a diamond from one square, then, on the next square, cut out the space around a diamond. Cut deeply enough to reveal the pattern, but no deeper. Continue, alternating, all the way around the pumpkin.

3. For the larger, floral motif, draw a petal within each square, alternating the diagonal orientation. Use a linoleum cutter or a chisel to scrape away a petal or the area surrounding a petal, alternating square by square. Cut deeply enough to reveal the pattern, but no deeper.

materials

'Lumina' pumpkins

moon and shooting star

Evoke the magic of a crystal-clear harvest night with a display of celestial images. Set them on a transom, along second-story windowsills, or atop two pedestals. This carving is simple enough for a beginner.

Other designs to fit the theme: ringed planets, clouds, a sun, even a rocket or a spaceship reminiscent of a retro fifties toy.

1. Draw the design on the surface of each pumpkin. Or, if you prefer, photocopy this picture to create templates for the two designs, enlarging them to the desired size. Tape the pattern to the pumpkins and, with a ballpoint pen or punch prick, trace over the outlines, scoring the line into the surface of the pumpkin. Remove the paper.

2. With a potter's tool or a chisel, scrape away the shape of the crescent, the star, and the star's trail, going approximately ¼ inch deep. (These creations are not meant to be illuminated, but you could adapt the idea for fully carved and lit pumpkins—carve all the way through or leave a layer of flesh to glow.)

materials

oval squash

elongated squash

flame, flicker, and glow

Before lighting the first real fire of the cold-weather months, outfit the hearth with pumpkins carved to resemble licks of flame. For a more pronounced effect, put more than one candle in each pumpkin. To build a bigger arrangement, set one or more pumpkins atop improvised risers of wide, flat pumpkins.

1. Cut a door in the back of each pumpkin. Cut a chimney vent behind each stem.

2. Draw flame shapes on the front of the pumpkins. Carefully carve away only the outline of the flame, as shown, being sure to leave the base of each flame attached.

3. With a linoleum cutter or a potter's tool, cut lines in the flesh within each flame just deeply enough to add flickering details, as shown. You may want to reach in through the back door with your noncarving hand to steady the flame and keep it from breaking off as you add these details.

4. Put candles inside the pumpkins and replace the doors.

materials

several tall pumpkins

candles

onion-dome lamps

The sliver-shaped windows ringing these lanterns perfectly frame the flames inside. Set them anywhere you'd normally use votive candles—a row down the center of a dinner table, a group on an entry-hall console, or one on a bathroom vanity. Set a coordinating saucer beneath each one for a decorative flourish—and to protect surfaces.

1. Cut a circle that's a bit larger than a votive candle from the bottom of each gourd and discard the circle. With a sturdy soup spoon, a grapefruit spoon, or an iced tea spoon, scrape out the seeds and the pulp.

2. Draw vertical sliver-shaped windows at even intervals around the gourd; adjust the proportions of the windows to complement the size and shape of each gourd. Cut out the shapes. (After you've cut out each window, you may want to trim their sides, angling the side walls outward to create wider openings for the light.)

3. Set a votive candle on each plate or saucer and place the gourd lantern over it.

materials

small to medium
lantern-shaped
gourds

votive candles

small plates or
saucers

window-
pane
lantern

One if by land, two if by broomstick? To greet little goblins or grown-up merrymakers, hang a lantern from a gateway arch or suspend one in the porch or front hall. A boxy squash, like this apple-shaped gourd, provides the optimum space for four-paned windows on both sides.

1. With masking tape, mark the design of a four-paned mullioned window on the front and back of the pumpkin (on each side, you'll apply six pieces of tape: one for the vertical muntin, one for the horizontal muntin, and four for each side of the frame). Cut out the resulting eight windowpanes. Working through the open windowpanes, remove the seeds and the pulp, being careful not to damage the muntins. Remove the tape.

2. In the base of the pumpkin, carve a circular well into which the glass votive holder will fit snugly (if you're not using the glass holder, carve a well to fit the candle). If you plan to hang the lantern, create a sling from the twine: Run two lengths of twine through the upper windowpanes, front to back; tie them together to another length, above the gourd, for hanging. You may need to cut little notches at the outside upper corners of each window to keep the sling in place.

materials

squarish squash (such as an apple gourd, similar to a gooseneck gourd)

¾-inch masking tape

cylindrical clear-glass votive holder, if desired

votive candle

twine, if desired

one- room pumpkin

A candle in a window is a welcoming beacon to nighttime visitors. Re-create the effect in miniature by making a gourd-roofed pumpkin house. Place one on a plant stand in a front window, make one for every window, or make a pair to sit at either end of a mantel. Think of this as autumn's answer to the gingerbread house.

1. Cut or break off the stem of the pumpkin.

2. Cut a door and a chimney vent in the back of the pumpkin. Scoop out the seeds and the pulp.

3. With a knife, cut a perfect square from the front of the pumpkin, adjusting its size and positioning it so that the flame of the votive candle will be visible. (Adapt this idea to a larger pumpkin by cutting out four, six, or nine window-panes and using a pillar or a taper candle.)

4. Position the gourd as the roof, making sure it will remain balanced. Lift it up, insert three toothpicks into its base, and attach it to the pumpkin by pressing the toothpicks into the pumpkin. Insert the candle and replace the back door.

materials

small pumpkin

turban squash

toothpicks

votive candle

polka-dot garlands

Whatever you do, don't connect these dots. Repetition is the name of the game. You can be a little bit formal and work a swagged design to echo antique upholstery-tack patterns. Or follow a loping curve, a zigzag, or a perfectly straight line around the circumference. This is one way to carve a lot of pumpkins very quickly—without mistakes!

1. Cut a door and a chimney vent in the back of the pumpkin. Scoop out the seeds and the pulp.

2. With an apple corer or a drill fitted with a large bit, create a "garland" of holes around the pumpkin, spacing them as evenly as possible. Make the holes in a scallop pattern or a gentle wave, as desired. Add a hole (or holes) on the door.

3. Put the candle inside the pumpkin and replace the door.

materials

pumpkins

candles

carving

♦

pairing off

If one is good, two must be better. Pairs of identical jack-o'-lanterns flanking a doorway, sideboard, mantel, or front gate always make an elegant statement. Another option is to devise a duo of complementary designs. Some suggestions: a cat and a mouse, easy-to-execute patterns of circles and squares, a flying bat and a crescent moon, the outlines of a standing coffin and a tombstone, and an acorn and an oak leaf.

faux pineappple finials

The gesture is real, but the symbols are an illusion. Pineapples, representing bounty and hospitality, are often depicted in carved-wood finials on furniture and fence posts. This pair of pumpkins masquerade as pineapples to beckon visitors along a path sculpted of autumn leaves. Boxwood clippings serve as the fronds.

1. Cut a door in the back of each pumpkin. Cut a chimney vent behind each stem. Scoop out the seeds and the pulp.

2. With masking tape, mark a cross-hatch design on the front and sides of each pumpkin, as shown above. Cut straight into the flesh of the pumpkins, about 1/2 inch deep (not all the way through), along the edges of the tape. Remove the tape.

3. Chisel and scrape out the channels that were under the tape, being careful not to carve all the way through.

4. In the middle of each diamond, carve a small, downward-pointing triangle. Cut deep, but not all the way through.

5. For the fronds, secure two bundles of boxwood clippings together with floral wire. Cut a hole in the top of each pumpkin to hold each bundle. Wrap the base of each bundle with moss for a soft finish, and insert the greens.

6. Put the candles or lights into the pumpkins and replace the back doors. Scrape more flesh from inside, if needed, to allow the light to show through.

materials

2 pineapple-shaped pumpkins

3/4-inch masking tape

boxwood or other evergreen branches

floral wire

sheet moss or sphagnum moss

candles, battery-operated lights, or outdoor-approved light sockets with 25- to 40-watt bulbs

all through the

Sea
son

Gourds and pumpkins are an art form unto themselves, with exquisite colors, innumerable complexions, and infinite profiles that make them as fascinating as any category of collectibles on the market. But unlike true objets d'art, these baubles appear, get scooped up by collectors, and then vanish with the season, not to reappear for many months. So don't restrict their decorating possibilities to Halloween. Start taking advantage of their simple beauty in late summer or early fall, long before the witches fly, and carry through to December, when reds and greens begin to replace autumn's earthy tones.

With the wealth of colors, textures, sizes, and shapes to choose from, all types of squash offer the beginnings of a stunning seasonal centerpiece, even before you step inside the house. Bring home a load of pumpkins to line the front steps or a porch railing. And for a true-blue country display? Cornstalks plus hay bales plus pumpkins is a classic formula that works every time.

Inside the front door, pile a collection of gourds in a yellowware bowl or a rustic basket for a cheery hall-table accent. In the dining room, group sugar pumpkins on a cake stand or in a wooden bread bowl, or intersperse white mini-pumpkins among ironstone displayed in a cupboard. Flank the front door

In the garden, on the porch, or in any room of the house, pumpkins and gourds lend instant autumnal charm and cheer. Feature them in their natural state, straight from the vine, or put them to work by turning them into vases, lollipop holders, candlesticks, or flower-studded orbs.

Usher in the season with a tumble of snow-white gourds, a parade of mismatched squashes along a mantel, or a single pumpkin doorstop.

or the fireplace with a pair of giant pumpkin watchdogs. Experiment with the contrast of rustic gourds in a formal compote or a glass vase. To round out the displays, weave in colorful autumn leaves, vines, acorns, pinecones, Indian corn, bundled sheaths of wheat, and other natural elements.

Once the harvest is under way, carving aficionados can indulge their craft all season long. To greet arriving guests at an autumn party and add drama to the front walkway, lay down a string of white outdoor Christmas lights (the kind with the large bulbs) and cover each bulb with a small, simply carved pumpkin lantern shade. Inscribe the word "Welcome" on a wide pumpkin and set it by the front door. Incorporate small pumpkins into dinner-table place settings—carved, they make wonderful place cards and double as party favors.

A pumpkin or squash can double as a sophisticated natural candlestick, a candelabra, or a generous candy bowl. With considerably less effort than it takes a potter to fashion a vase, you can turn a warty gourd or a wonderfully weird-looking pumpkin into a conversation-piece flower holder. Simply slice off the top, scoop out the seeds and the pulp, fill it with water, and add seasonal flowers and branches of colorful leaves and shapely seedpods.

pumpkin and squash cuisine

roasted pumpkin seeds

This crunchy-salty-toasty snack is addictive and also good for you. Try roasting the seeds of other winter squash, too. Acorn squash seeds, for example, though smaller than those of the pumpkin, are plumper and surprisingly meaty.

Heat the oven to 350°F. Rinse the raw seeds thoroughly to remove the pulp, rub them in a cloth towel to remove remaining fibers, and pat them dry. Toss them with just enough olive or vegetable oil to coat them lightly, then salt them lightly and toss. Spread the seeds in a single layer on a baking sheet. Bake about 15 minutes, or until the seeds reach the desired crispness and have a golden-brown color. If you crave an infusion of spiciness, try adding one—or a combination—of the following along with the salt: chili powder, cumin, curry powder, cinnamon, or cayenne pepper (just a pinch).

roasted squash

Regular jack-o'-lantern pumpkins do not make for tasty eating, but sugar pumpkins and many other kinds of winter squash do. Acorn, butternut, and sweet dumpling squash are especially delicious. Keep them on hand as decorations (uncarved, of course) until it's time to turn them over to the kitchen.

Heat the oven to 350°F. Cut the squash in half through the stem end and scoop out the seeds and the pulp. Rub the cut surface with olive or vegetable oil, sprinkle with salt and pepper, and place, cut side down, in a greased baking dish. Roast about 1 hour, or until the skin can be easily pierced with a fork and the flesh is tender. Depending on the size of the squash, serve in the shell or scoop out the meat and make a puree.

For a variation, roast the squash over several unpeeled cloves of garlic. If making a puree, adjust the seasonings and try adding a bit of maple syrup or ground spices.

farmstand
trick-or-treat
bowl
Set out candy for trick-or-treaters or Halloween party guests in a pumpkin-shell container. A bed of hay, straw, or leaves on a big round platter creates a more finished look. A little sign suggesting portion control will draw attention to the candy supply, but it's unlikely that anyone will heed the message.

1. Cut a wide opening in the top of the pumpkin. Scoop out the seeds and the pulp. Rinse the inside of the pumpkin with cool water and pat dry.

2. To keep the candy out of contact with the pumpkin flesh, line the interior of the pumpkin with foil or set a bowl inside the cavity.

3. Cut vellum paper in wide strips and roll it over lengthwise several times, crumpling it slightly to resemble a pie crust. Secure it to the cut rim of the pumpkin with floral u-pins (insert two pins at each point, overlapping them at different angles so they won't easily pull out). Adjust the "crust," and fill the bowl with candy.

materials

large flattish pumpkin, such as 'Rouge Vif d'Étampes' (Cinderella)

foil or a bowl that fits inside the pumpkin

vellum paper

floral u-pins

easy party decor

Armed with a drill and the right size bits, you'll be able to make a good supply of seasonal party decorations in no time flat. Sturdy little sugar pumpkins become ideal candleholders and lollipop centerpieces. Use votive candles instead of, or in combination with, tapers. Outdoors, you may need to slip a glass hurricane over each pumpkin candlestick.

1. For the candleholder, gently pull or cut off the stem. With a drill or an apple corer, cut a hole straight down into the top of the pumpkin into which the candle will fit snugly. If necessary, scrape the hole to adjust it to the candle. Insert the candle and tie a sprig of seeded eucalyptus around it, securing it as if you were starting to tie a knot.

2. For the candy stand, drill small holes at different angles around the top and sides of the pumpkin, wherever (and as many) as desired. Insert the lollipop sticks.

materials

sugar pumpkins

taper candles and/or votive candles

seeded eucalyptus

lollipops

entertaining

✦

one for the road

At the end of an autumn party, send each guest home with a sweet favor. Fill a tray near the door with small sugar pumpkins, write guests' names on manila tags, and tie them to the stems. For children, fill small glassine bags with candy corn and cinch them around amusingly curled gourds with twine or orange ribbon.

shades
of fall.
topiary

The harvest of autum squashes yields so many subtle, distinctive colors: bluish grays, frosted taupes, milky whites. It's easy to go a little overboard at the farmstand when you come across a gorgeous array. If you choose varieties that are fairly flat, stacking is enough to transform them into artful displays.

1. Gently break or cut off the stems of the pumpkins to be used in the tower. Decide on your stacking order.

2. For the topmost pumpkin, cut off the top and scoop out the seeds and the pulp.

3. Reserve the pumpkin destined for the top. Drill a dowel-diameter hole straight down through the center of each pumpkin's top; turn over each pumpkin and drill the same size hole straight down the bottom center. Cut the dowel to the height of the tower plus the depth of the urn. Insert the dowel into the soil or sand in the urn and press to make it secure. Slide each pumpkin down the dowel (you may need to wiggle each one as you line up the holes and then wipe away any seeds and pulp that are pressed out during the process). Attach the hollowed-out pumpkin to the top pumpkin with three or four toothpicks or pieces of skewer. Fill this vase with the greenery.

materials

a variety of flattish pumpkins

long wooden dowel

garden urn filled with soil or sand

toothpicks or bamboo skewers

hardy greenery, such as the leafy top of a Brussels sprout stalk or other autumn leafy greens

gourd candle-holders

When it comes to gourds and pumpkins, the fire doesn't always have to glow from within. For entertaining or simply to dress the house for the season, use a gourd with every candle. Knobby, bumpy gourds might be reminiscent of those classic, deliberately decorative wax drips on a Chianti-bottle candlestick.

1. For a double-decker display, as shown opposite, remove the stems from both gourds. Drill a hole in the top gourd to hold the candle. With the bottom gourd facing bottom-up (to take advantage of the flatter end of the gourd), secure the gourds together with three toothpicks or cut pieces of bamboo skewer (use a thin nail or a drill to make the holes if a gourd is too hard). Pull the gourds slightly apart, tuck in several sprigs of seeded eucalyptus between them, and press them together again. Fill the urn with moss, set the double decker into the urn, and insert the candle.

2. For the candlesticks, as shown above, break the stem off each gourd or pumpkin. With a drill, cut a hole in the top of each gourd big enough to hold the candle. Press the gourd on the candlestick's spike and insert the candle. If the candle won't fit, shave the edge of the hole; if it is too loose, wrap its base with a strip of plastic wrap or modeling clay to hold it securely.

materials

small and medium gourds

pronged candlesticks

metal or wire urn

seeded eucalyptus

sheet moss or sphagnum moss

toothpicks or bamboo skewers

dotted gooseneck hurricane

The gooseneck gourd, so aptly named because of its fowl-like appearance, is a marvelously sculptural object in its untouched state. These gourds grow in countless expressive postures. Here, one becomes a candle shade, its speckled exterior enhanced by holes drilled in several sizes.

1. Choose a gourd that will stand upright on its base. Cut a hole approximately 3 inches wide in the base of the gourd. Discard the base and scoop out the seeds and the pulp from the gourd.

2. Drill holes of several sizes at regular intervals around the bulbous portion of the squash. Arrange the leaves around the plate, place the candle in the middle, and set the gourd over the candle.

materials

large gooseneck gourd

votive candle

plate

large green leaves

decorating

✦

plated pumpkins

A plump jack-o'-lantern can't do much damage on the front steps. But if you're displaying your creations on surfaces that could be marred by moisture—especially wood furniture—you may want to slip a plate or a saucer beneath the pumpkin. A leaf-covered platter, a copper plant tray, or a chipped vintage compote suitable for ghoulish servings could all be incorporated as stylish elements of the display.

pumpkin patch wreath

One of the great country pleasures is without doubt the magical afternoon search for just the right treasures in a great big pumpkin patch. Here, the strange beauty of one of those viny fields is tidied and tweaked in an elegant autumn centerpiece. And unlike a vase of flowers, this arrangement will last for many weeks.

1. With the wreath form laying flat on a work surface, cover the entire top of the form with moss, securing it with lengths of floral wire (position bits of moss over the wire to obscure it). Alternatively, attach the moss to the form with hot glue.

2. Insert two toothpicks or cut pieces of bamboo skewer (no longer than the thickness of the wreath form) into the bottom of each pumpkin. Spacing the pumpkins evenly around the top of the wreath, press each one into place, anchoring the toothpicks or skewers into the vines of the form (you may need to wiggle them into place).

3. Position the wreath on the table. Place some moss inside the hurricane, add the candle, and place it in the center of the wreath.

materials

5 or 6 little pumpkins or gourds

16- to 18-inch grapevine wreath form

sheet moss or sphagnum moss

fine-gauge green floral wire or hot-glue gun

bamboo skewers or toothpicks

glass hurricane

pillar candle

place-
card
monograms

Carve a personalized coat of arms or a simple rendering of initials on a miniature pumpkin for every guest at an autumn dinner party. This is a sweet touch for the Thanksgiving table, of course, but for a frightful Halloween alternative, surround the initials with a tombstone outline and, to be extra wicked, add "R.I.P."

1. If you're using a very small sugar pumpkin, as shown opposite, draw initials and a frame (we used a shield shape) on the pumpkin. With a citrus zester or a linoleum cutter, cut out the letters and the frame.

2. If you're using a 'Jack Be Little,' as shown above, draw one initial into each of the ridges. This variety of pumpkin can be quite hard, so it's best to carve with a linoleum cutter.

3. For a tassel, tie a piece of natural or green garden twine around each stem, trim to desired length, and fray the ends.

materials

very small sugar and/or 'Jack Be Little' pumpkins

garden twine

carving
♦

writing
class

If you're feeling eloquent, put your pumpkin to work as a writing tablet. Wielding a zester or a linoleum cutter instead of a pen, you can inscribe a special message to a loved one, scrawl spooky words for a Halloween display ("Skull!" "Howl!" "Screech!"), or create a Thanksgiving "greeting card" to deliver to a friend's doorstep.

buffet
menu
banners

Identify the dishes of a fall potluck dinner or a Thanksgiving buffet with hand-lettered signposts rising from colorful gourds. Use the same assemblage to list the names and prices of goodies at a bake sale or to hold table numbers at a fall wedding or dinner dance. Use colored vellum for the most luminous banners.

1. Select one gourd for each dish on your buffet table. Decide how you want to arrange the gourd, making sure it will remain stable. Leaving the gourd in that position, pierce it once with an awl at what is now the top, tapping gently with a hammer if necessary. Push the sharp end of the skewer into the hole in the gourd.

2. Cut out paper rectangles approximately 2½ inches by 4 inches and write the name of one dish in the center of each. With a ⅛-inch hole punch, make one hole above and one below the dish name. Slide each card onto a skewer.

materials

medium gourds

colored vellum or other stiff paper

markers

6-inch bamboo skewers

cheddar
corn bread

rosemary
chicken

lemon mustard
brussel sprouts

mixed autumn bouquet

With the top trimmed off and the insides scooped out, a generously sized autumn squash becomes a natural vase that's completely integral to the arrangement. Splashes of purple—here, stalks of ornamental kale—freshen the expected seasonal palette of green, gold, and orange.

1. Cut 3 or 4 inches from the top of the squash, slicing straight across. Scoop out the seeds and the pulp. Rinse out the inside and fill with water.

2. Create the arrangement: Begin with the kale, since its stalks are thicker than the other materials, then add the autumn branches, and finish with the eucalyptus, adjusting until you are satisfied with the proportion and fullness of the bouquet. To protect furniture, set the vase on a plate or platter.

materials

large, upright squash or pumpkin with a level base

stalks of ornamental kale

branches of autumn leaves

branches of seeded eucalyptus

decorating

✦

autumn bouquets

Coordinate the materials of your arrangement with your pumpkin or gourd vase. For example, a bold orange pumpkin might hold branches of flame-colored leaves, tawny Indian corn with the husks pulled back like petals, red and orange dahlias, and bittersweet. To ensure watertightness, you can line the pumpkin with a plastic container; insert floral foam if you want to anchor a tightly composed bouquet.

flower-banded pompons

After summer's abundance, late-autumn flowers almost demand special treatment. For a change of pace from a traditional floral centerpiece, small sugar pumpkins become unusual flower holders for tiny chartreuse chrysanthemums. Adorn every orb the same way, or vary the axis of the encircling bands of blossoms.

1. Draw a dotted design on the pumpkin surface, spacing the dots so that when the stems are inserted the blossoms will be positioned shoulder to shoulder, as shown above. With an awl or a nail, punch a hole in each dot.

2. Trim the flower stems to about ½ inch each. Insert a stem into each punch hole.

materials

small round sugar pumpkins

tiny green chrysanthemums

decorating
◆

instant impact

With extra thought and planning at the farmstand or market, you can select an array of gourds and pumpkins for display as carefully as you would flowers for a bouquet. Then, once you're home, superb arrangements will seem to materialize on their own. Buy green, green-and-white, and white gourds, then group them by color on a three-tiered dessert stand. For a subtle, elegant infusion of the season in a formal room, choose exclusively white gourds, including 'Lumina' and 'Baby Boo' pumpkins.

lidded
flowerpot
tableau

In days past, hollow dried gourds were pressed into service as water dippers. Freshly harvested winter squashes can be scooped out and filled with water to double as flower vases. Choose a variety of gourds and flowers to complement one another in a grouped arrangement. Here, from the left, are ornamental kale, calla lilies, and tulips—a flower-stall luxury this time of year.

1. Slice off the top inch or so of each squash, pumpkin, or gourd, cutting straight across, and save the lids. Remove the seeds and the pulp. Rinse out the interiors.

2. Fill each vase with water and arrange the flowers, one variety to each vase. To help keep them steady and to create a naturalistic scene, set the filled vases on a bed of moss and place the lids to the sides of the vases. If you wish, lay down a protective layer, such as plastic wrap, on the surface where you plan to set the grouping. To create a mess-free, movable tableau, fill a medium to large platter with moss and arrange the grouping on it.

materials

assorted pumpkins and winter squashes

flowering kale, calla lilies, and tulips, or other flowers

sheet moss or sphagnum moss

gourd-topped candelabra

With a little imagination, you can use a wide, flat pumpkin as the base for a dramatic and stylish candelit centerpiece. A creamy-colored specimen and a cascading pile of snow-white gourds hint at the approaching winter holiday season.

1. Carefully break or cut the stem off the pumpkin. Using a bit that's just a fraction smaller than the diameter of the candles, drill five evenly spaced holes in a ring around the top of the pumpkin, drilling straight down 1 to 2 inches.

2. Insert the candles into the holes; scrape the openings a tiny bit if necessary. If the holes are too big, secure the candle by wrapping the base with a strip of plastic wrap or a small amount of modeling glue.

3. Arrange the greenery on top of the pumpkin, allowing it to trail down the sides, and secure it in place with floral u-pins. Arrange the gourds on top of the greenery, securing each gourd to the pumpkin with a toothpick, if necessary, for stability. Set several gourds on the table, around the base of the pumpkin, to enhance the cascading effect.

materials

1 large flattish pumpkin

5 taper candles

seeded eucalyptus or other greenery

floral u-pins

toothpicks

assorted small white and pale-colored gourds

Acknowledgments

The creative team would like to thank
Thomas and Terri Holmes of Holmquest Farms,
Hudson, New York; Mary Mullane;
Warner Johnson; and Craig Fitt.